SUCCEED

A Handbook on Structuring Managerial Thought

by John Allen

SP
Synergetic Press, Inc.

Published by Synergetic Press, Inc.
Post Office Box 689, Oracle, Arizona 85623
24 Old Gloucester Street, London WC1 3AL

Book design by Kathleen Dyhr.
Typesetting by Synergetic Press on Studio Software.

ISBN 0-907791-042

Printed in the United States of America by Arizona Lithographers (Tucson).

Contents

Acknowledgments

The author first began studies of structure with Plato under the guidance of the great Swiss Hegelian, Professor Gustav Mueller, aided by the enthusiasm of Mueller's main student, Mr. Ben Epperson. After Hegel and Kant, and Hegel's great students, Marx and Engels, the trail led to Pythagoras and his theory of the objective reality of numbers, Aristotle and his four causes, the Parmenidean monad, the Heraclitean dyad, the Buddhist five-term logic, Zen paradox (dyad), Buckminster Fuller with his triads, tetrads, and hexagons, Einstein's four dimensions, Beethoven's Quartets, the theological triad, projective geometry and equilibria systems at Mining Engineering School, Gurdjieff's Laws of three and seven, Ouspensky's six dimensions of recurrence, the Sufic Eight, Lawrence Durrell's Quartet and later his Quintet, and John Bennett's Systematics. Bennett had also studied all of the above except perhaps the Buddhist and Zen and Durrell, and in 1971 in exchange for my demonstrating theater exercises at his project at Sherborne House passed on to me for my free use both his published and unpublished work on what he called Systematics.

The author believes that this publication is the first time that these structures with their mighty power to organize the attention have ever been presented in a completely practical form, although they will be practical only for those individuals who actually do possess an attention capable of the discipline of advanced self-organization and who furthermore possess the proper field of action for data and feedback, namely, an ongoing enterprise. This possession of both inner discipline and external power is rare. His experience has been that all others will either undervalue this knowledge plus practice because they can get but little use from it themselves and will dismiss it as unsubstantiated assertions, or they will overvalue it and make an icon of it because they will feel its power but realize it is not for them as they are and are likely-to-be. Others who cannot yet deal with the material but see possibilities within it will sense that it is best to put the book upon their shelves and prepare themselves until they can read it with profit.

Of course the enterprise might be the rehabilitation of a nation as Lincoln and de Gaulle, the creation of a vast new technics as Ford, von Braun, and Edison, the operation of a farm, a ranch, a research institute, the managing of one's life as Walt Whitman, exploration of a new frontier, writing intelligent software, curing the sick, challenging the healthy, whatever so long as one takes the total responsibility and deals with life itself in all its many vectors.

That the author believes that this is the first time these structures have been presented in public practical form does not mean that he does not believe that they have been understood at perhaps several times and places in human history; only that then they were applied by schools that kept their craft a guarded secret, and that they were applied mainly in the fields of psychological transformation and transmissions of this wisdom by means of Art. Indeed without the clues found in those areas, and the names da Vinci, Karnak, and Naqshband must stand for what is being referred to, all of his acknowledgments to the truth fragments of philosophers in the first paragraph must render the matter more rather than less mysterious. He believes they are practical among other reasons because he applied them to the setting up and operating of numerous corporations and projects in a total of over 30 different cultures and with many different types of individuals. Of course, anyone can see that this assertion in no way constitutes even an approximation to scientific proof of the belief, nor does the author claim any scientific truth, and indeed metaphysics must rely totally on ever-changing perception and action, not formulas, to validate its structures and eros. The colleagues who assisted him in this experimental endeavor are the true heroes, if this book is indeed found useful. If it is found to be not really necessary, the more heroic they, who succeeded in spite of the extra burden.

basically failed as stewards of the abundant life, through overuse and misuse of force by one and dogma by the other; and three, that economic management faces an equally catastrophic result because, failing to use structures of thought, its managers often associatively, logically, or dialectically plunder a society's natural resources, biospheric and personal, seeking profit by not counting costs except those they are directly forced to pay, for example not counting waste disposal -- human, informational, conceptual, material, and energetic -- when it can "dump" them on the environment. Although such policies may lead to success, they cannot *succeed.* To assist managers to evolve an ecological orientation, the author does not propose to make managers become ecologists, rather, he proposes to assist managers to become ecological by fulfilling properly their econiche in the biosphere, using the power of structured thought which contains the power of direction.

He has full confidence that use of structured thought will show managers who have reached success how to succeed, and that succeed means to make a more complex, creative future, and that a more complex, creative future will find itself aligned, as always in the past, with that great system we know as evolution which now includes more and more of the ever-innovative technical system, as yet in its inchoate beginnings but already clearly destined to be managed to beautify a prosperous Earth and to voyage space itself.

THE MONAD

Notes

Each of the structures requires a definite discipline to enable them to unite the qualities and quantities of a given situation into understanding, that power which gives the capacity to succeed. If any of the structures sound simple to the reader's doubtless well-educated brain, please reflect upon the difficulty of putting them into practice in order to appreciate their complexity.

The discipline of the monad requires the manager not to evaluate any item within or without the monad as any more or less important than any other item, and to locate the item as definitively in or out. When the reader recalls the near-incessant questioning of daily existence -- this or that? -- he will reflect that all of this or that type of thought presupposes a difference and that keen discipline indeed would be required to view a large number of items as of equal importance in a monad of urgent concern. The ultimate expressible realization of monadic religion is that "this, too, is the will of Allah", or that lilies, sparrows, and men are equally watched by the eye of God (the monad of the Creator: the created world). Only a handful of saints or masters have been acknowledged to have achieved such inspired impartiality, and only after years of toil upon their attention and emotion. To be sure, the creator of an enterprise has created a much smaller world than the universe, but the basic difficulty remains as acute for the one called to the path of action as for the one called to the path of contemplation: to overcome preference. Since overcoming preference is repugnant to human nature as it is born, discipline must be invoked and practiced.

First, the manager draws a large circle or, if he is a keen visualizer, imagines one in his mental attention.

Inside the circle he begins to enumerate all the items that "belong in his monad", for example in his corporation: marketing, production, finance, organization, research, development, Joe Welsh the President, Sally Rand his secretary, etc. These items should be placed at random, and each contemplated briefly, impartially, as equally important. When he has filled the circle to the end of the first bout of enumeration, he adds a black box which represents all of the as-yet and some-that-never-will-be enumerated items belonging to the manager's monad. If the process continues past the ability to hold each item as equally important and one begins to say, "oh these aren't so important," then one has gone forward, but unconsciously so, to the dyad with the polarity gradient of important/not-so-important. Great executives have always been legendary for their ability to deal with everyone from the President to their shoeshine boy, with everything from billions to the right tip for a cup of coffee, giving each that same moment of 100%

They can be metaphorically visualized as a series of Chinese boxes nesting inside each other. The manager who tries to use these structures with inadequate discipline and makes a too-small monad loses even that ordinary share of practicality he once possessed and is hurled, DeLorean-like, into the hell of the half-baked big ideas, a "dreamer-who-failed".

Notes

The manager, however, who conscientiously ponders his way through his monad, and forces himself to regard, say, his expense account, his secretary, his suit, his drinking pattern, his office furniture, as equal in importance to the company policy, the president, his chief vice-presidential competitor, and the tariff will commence to gain that most valuable of qualities for the leader who wishes to succeed, impartiality. This manager will not lose battles because of the nail lacking in the shoe of a horse, or a glitch in the computer. Nor will he lose the war by not paying attention to the new scientific discovery in the lab. He will understand, for a starter, that anything in the monad has importance and that nothing in the monad has total importance. Insofar as he can complete the monadic exercise, he can view all events from the "standpoint of eternity", outside time's entropy. He attains the first stage of direct perception. Please note the "insofar as he can". In the monad, the mathematical representation of eternity, as in heaven, one of the poetic representations of eternity, the widow's mite counts for as much as the finest linen and oils from the rich. The legendary Sid Richardson, for example, counted as friends to be wooed with equal attention, the telephone operator in West Texas who kept him up on who called whom, and Franklin Roosevelt who kept him up on what oil men could get from Washington and for how much of what.

How long should you make your monad list, both inner and outer? As long as it interests you. No man could ever finish to objective completion a single monad, either of his corporation, or of his life, or of his life's ambitions, or of whatever. Each real monad represents a man's own work, a successive approximation to reality. Each monad objectively contains an infinity of items; in the third discipline of the monad, the manager must decide to let the "black box" hold all items which do not interest him as yet. Let them emerge as his interest deepens. Put them back in as his interest lessens.

The manager draws a new circle each time he changes the content of his monad, and if you keep a record of your successive efforts you will possess an interesting history of the fluctuations of your monad.

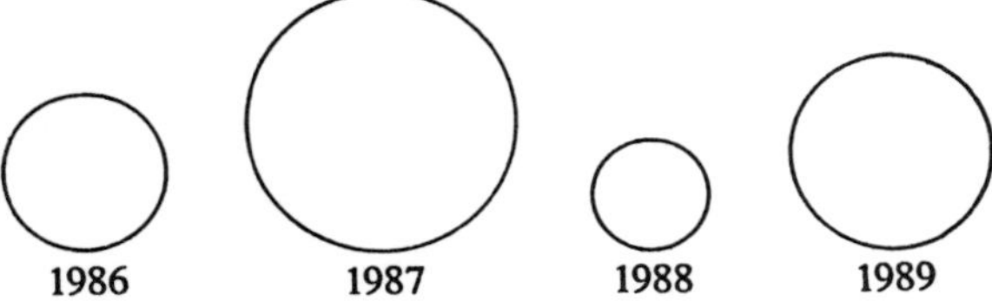

The Monad

Notes

No monad exists apart from my interested attention. I create mine, when I do, and you, yours, when you do, and when we turn our interest elsewhere they disappear from the phenomenological or actual world unlike chairs. Fortunately their energy conserves itself in potentiality so they can be summoned to re-appear. Mental creations, they perform reciprocal maintenance in their creators, giving the creator understanding in exchange for his interest and they give much to prevent his interest going elsewhere, because like vanished god-symbols, they eventually disappear without the input of their creators.

If the monad does not interest you, it disappears, although of course its elements, your circle, black boxes, and items may persist as images on paper, or even as words in a bored and therefore literalist attention.

The manager makes monads, and continues on, if he does, to make dyads, triads, etc., in order to increase his *capacity* to do; what the manager *actually* does will still accomplish itself by words, posture, gesture, numbers, orders, signs, sweat, costumes, tools, etc., all the techniques that can be learned from observation, from others, from self-critique. Nonetheless, the capacity of the manager wielding his devices will make his efforts the more comprehensive and his discrimination the more penetrating.

Try the exercise:

1. Pick the monad that most interests you.
2. Draw the circle.
3. Put a black box inside and outside the circle.
4. List first the items of the inside or outside that interest you and then quit when your interest flags, drops to being unable to maintain the discipline of regarding them all as equally important.
5. List the items of the other, inside or outside, etc. as in 4.
6. Contemplate your results, from enumerating, in and outing, and black boxing.
7. Put it aside and take it up again to speed up steps from 1 -- 5 to contemplate again from time to time until adding or subtracting items, or until you become aware of an ineluctable certainty that A is more important than B and that no questions in your mind exist about that relative importance, and also that some connection has emerged between A and B. For example, a manager may in his monad see sales becoming more important than production; they are connected by delivery, cash in one direction, things or services in the other.
8. At this point move on to THE DYAD.

The Monad

Notes

THE DYAD

Notes

The manager needs to contemplate the basic form of the situation but he also needs the force to deal with the situation. From the monad with its infinite capacity for extension, the manager moves on to structure intensity into force with the dyad. And here he faces a finite capacity for intensity. If too much intensity, he explodes, cracks up. If too little, he goes dull, freezes, blanks out.

When a manager says "I feel comfortable with that...", this signals that he has just, unconsciously perhaps, completed a survey of his monad and been able to include the item in. However, it shows that he has not considered the dyad because attention to this structure causes and can only cause discomfort.

A dyad cannot be created just by juxtaposing two items; they must become a dipole, that is, connected. No matter how a dipole twists and turns or is twisted and turned the two ends remain connected, like a cane, or a sword, or a pencil, the end that unites connected with the end that erases. The connection is what keeps up the separation, one end of the cane for the mind, the other for the hand. Heat at one end of thermometer and cold at the other end. The dyad produces a strain that nothing can relieve, like love, except when an explosion occurs that severs the connection, like a break-up in love, or when it freezes over, like repressed anger in love. Then we are left with an exploded monad, or with a monad frozen into tyrannical rigidity.

How to manage the dyad? How to gain the intensity that the manager needs to investigate his form, the force to deepen his penetration of the situation?

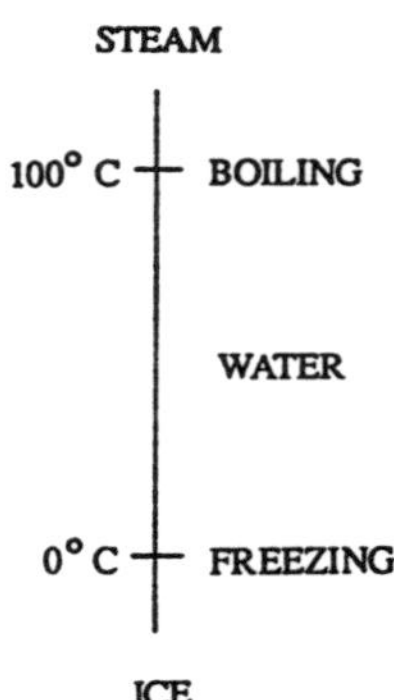

The manager takes heed of the dyad hot-cold for an aligning analogy. He sets up a negative feedback so that when the temperature approaches boiling, it is driven back down, and when about to freeze, driven back up. Forcing himself to deal with near-explosion and near-rigidity, near chaos and near order, but never succumbing to the temptation to destroy the liquid, water, that connects boiling and freezing, steam and ice, thoroughly uncomfortable, he puts himself through the internally adaptive paces that his brother executive, carefully keeping the temperature at 23 degrees C plus or minus one, comfortable in his monad, fearful of exploding or freezing, avoids. However, he gains knowledge of all the properties of "liquid water", he gains capacity to see possibilities his comfortable brother will never know.

Notes

Neither does he explode or freeze, go out of control, destroy his monad. And with the force of this intensity, he begins to perceive directly, to see:

Priorities, the dyad of more urgent and less urgent;

Rulers and ruled, the dyad of power;

The risks and opportunities, the dyad of enterprise.

The monad as he scans it begins to writhe with dipoles, just as a drop of water, put under the gaze of a microscope, reveals writhing amoeba. The dipoles began to grow distinct, he sees which dyads cause him to experience the most intense strain, to approach his explosion point and warn him to turn back, which dyads are about to rigidify and need warming impacts, and which dyads have been almost shut down into tepid suburban boredom. Also, he sees the great dyads that any aim must generate:

Loyalty and self-interest;

Good and evil;

Friends and enemies;

and he sees these, not as abstract, boring generalizations devoid of practical content, but as living, even flaming dipoles, each containing enough nuclear power to fuel his monad onward past obstacles once seeming too mighty to think about, let alone challenge, because of fear of blowing-up his whole situation and being cast into the freak side streets of failure, or the fear of being frozen out of the action.

Try the exercise:

1) Pick the dyad from the items in your monad that makes you the most uncomfortable. In addition, apply at least one of the six dyads given above, for example: *loyalty and self-interest.*
2) Draw the line.
3) Put a boiling line horizontal near the top, and a freezing line near the bottom.
4) In your imagination push your monad's location on that line as near to the boiling point as you can, that is, imagine what you could do to raise the situation to that level of self-interest, then quickly reverse and

imagine your monad's location on that line as near to the freezing point as you can, that is, imagine what you could do to raise the situation to that level of loyalty.

Notes

5) In your imagination (unless, of course it's actually happening), push your monad into the exploding region, let's say when self-interest becomes not only the only criterion but is even Machiavellianly calculated, computed by zero-sum gamed computers, then reverse and push your monad into the freezing region, where loyalty becomes not only the only criterion but is pushed to the point of extinction of all independent thought, emotion, sensation, and judgment. Reverse again. Do the same on your dyad drawn directly from your monad's items, as sales and production or finance and the workers.

6) Contemplate your results.

7) Put those two dyads aside and do the two dyads most troubling to you. Work on these next two dyads until you create an intensity that will keep your attention moving ceaselessly, uncomfortably between the dipoles, culminating with the direct experiencing that (for example):

loyalty contains self-interest, self-interest loyalty;
good contains evil, evil good;
the more important contains less important, and the less important more important;
friends contain enemies, enemies friends;
risks contain opportunities, and opportunities risks;
finance contains workers, workers finance;
sales contains production, production sales;

or, if you used other dyads, that A contains B, and B contains A. Push this feeling until you dare not do anything because any extra step will lead to disaster.

8) At this point without losing any of the force developed, move on to THE TRIAD.

The Dyad

Notes

THE TRIAD

Notes

Now, experiencing form and force, the form comfortable, the force uncomfortable, the manager structuring his thought can move his sharpened attention to the triad where he encounters the dynamism of ever-shifting relationships. Of course, being a manager in the scientific-technical revolution world, he has been aware that he acts in an externally dynamic world. But this experienced self-created dynamism lives inside him, making a fast-changing, adaptive, strategic thinking, a thinking moving quickly enough to begin to deal as an equal with the quick world, evolving a quickening synergy.

Let us call the three elements of the triad 1,2,3.

Mathematically we can see that there are six possible arrangements:

1	1	2	2	3	3
2	3	1	3	1	2
3	2	3	1	2	1

If we call the monad the way to structure our objective or field of action, and the dyad the way to structure our policies to deal with this field of action, then we can call the triad the way to structure our strategy to arrange the battles that we wish to fight to maintain or better the position of our field of action in alignment with policies.

Let us call 1, in words, the assertion "thus-and so". Let us call 2, in words, the reception of "thus-and-so", namely yes/no/somewhat depending on the time, place, people, and skills involved. Let us call 3, in words, the purpose or results that we wish to obtain or realize we will get in any event from a particular thus-and-so and yes/no/somewhat.

Remember in the monad, the manager obtained no results, the manager contemplated a self-painted portrait of his reality. In the dyad, the manager obtained no results, the manager accumulated force, potential, capacity, not yet discharged. Neither step deals directly with any results.

The triad shows the manager six *strategies* to obtain results, and also how to deal with these results.

In a *1-2-3* strategy, the manager brings thus-and-so directly against reception. "Do thus-and-so now!" Whether the answer comes yes/no/somewhat the situation becomes bigger, the situation expands. Everyone "hangs on the answer". Implications immediately flood into the manager's attention. He must "go out" or "follow-up" on the results. His universe enlarges. If it enlarges too greatly, he will lose his grip on it, it runs away from him. Ford expanded and expanded until GM took the growth curve away from him. GM expanded and expanded until the Japanese took the growth curve away. Germany expanded to the East for a thousand years until the Russians took it all back plus some. A strategy of endless expansion sooner or later ends, often in retreat, sometimes in disastrous retreat such as Napoleon's retreat from Moscow.

Notes

Durable long-term growth nations such as Russia, the United States and China have known how to couple 1-2-3 expanding triads with 2-1-3 or concentrating triads. Lenin gave up the Ukraine to Germany in the treaty of Brest-Litovsk (taken back when the German expansion collapsed on the Western Front), Finland and the Baltic States got independence, Ukrainians were given to Poland. All except Finland were re-acquired in the next German collapse. The American expansion knew how to give up the Phillipines, leave Vietnam, give back Okinawa, the Panama Canal Zone, how to take nothing from the World War I victory. China retreated two thousand miles before the Japanese as it had retreated in the past before Russia, Britain, Germany, and the Mongols. IBM stayed out of the personal computer market for a long time. IBM left India.

In the 2-1-3 strategy, the manager begins with yes/no/somewhat, then goes to thus-and-so and afterwards looks at his diminished, and therefore more concentrated monad. However, if the 2-1-3 strategy (divestiture, say) lasts too long, the manager winds up with "Little England", or with little oil. Ross Perot sells out totally, a big 2-1-3, and capital concentrates into his hands, but can he build another empire, 1-2-3, with it? Steven Job creates Apple, 1-2-3 then concentrates, 2-1-3, its power into a new management, but he himself got kicked out as part of the main concentration process to prepare a new sales expansion. Israel represents a giant 2-1-3 from the Diasporic 1-2-3 expansions, but the weakness of this 2-1-3 strategy carried too far is that now one loss can destroy so much. All the expansion eggs wind up in one concentrated basket, and that basket, no matter how watched can be dropped. Nonetheless, this was exactly Andrew Carnegie's stategy, "put all your eggs into one basket, and then watch that basket". His basket was U.S. Steel, which he sold before dying or big taxes came, and concentrated still further into his charities.

In the 1-3-2 or efficiency strategy, the manager has his "thus-and-so" but he carefully goes over the "range of possible results" before he commits to "yes/no/somewhat", thereby he enables himself to adjust the 1 very close to the 2 even if they were quite different to begin with. For the 1-2-3 strategy to work well, clearly the 1 and 2 must fit like a key in the lock, and where this fit seems uncertain the 1-3-2 triad should prove a better strategy. 1-3-2 neither expands nor diminishes the monad, but it makes more efficient, more easy, the operation of what already exists. The manager "learns to live with the situation". He "rolls with the

Notes

punches". His operations go as smoothly "as a Swiss watch". The strategy of efficiency carried to a mindless end produces the faceless ruler. Nobody trusts the manager. "He would sell his grandmother for a profit (or power)." That is, to say, the manager always trims and cuts his thus-and-so to stay even with his yes/no/somewhat.

If the rest of the world were standing still, this strategy might perhaps survive being the only one used. But, fatally, in a changing, expanding world one's monad becomes relatively smaller to more evolutionary monads. The 2 becomes ever more *no* and ever less *yes*. The 1 diminishes. Icahn and Pickens float like sharks over the efficient corporation doing its own thing better and better, getting fatter, its 1-3-2 ready to be swallowed up at the right moment by someone else's expansion 1-2-3. The Soviet Union slowly becomes a raw material producer for Western Europe as its industry lags behind expanding competitors although it's governed ever more efficiently since the fall of Stalin. Undoubtedly it should have gone into more of a concentration 2-1-3 than the brief Khruschevian thaw before switching to 1-3-2 efficiency and rid itself of more of the untoward consequences of a truly magnificent 1-2-3* than the worst excesses in Siberia and the Austrian occupation.

The 2-3-1 strategy begins with the yes/no/somewhat, considers the range of possible results, and then says thus-and-so. This strategy produces a reliable image, and perhaps even reliability. A Bayer Aspirin commercial shows exactly this triad, how its product reliably cures certain symptoms. In fact all brand names endeavor to use this strategy. The manager using it becomes well-known, one calls Red Adair to put out one's fiery oil well. One goes to an 007 movie for a reliable escape, while 007 himself uses all the reliable brands. The manager who reliably knows how "to cut the bone" gets called in to "save sinking corporations". Japanese products establish their quality control reliability, and one "buys Japanese", actually the reliable quality. American engineers developed the methods, but American managers became obsessed with the quick payoffs of the strategies of expansion and efficiency. The problem with the strategy of reliability, carried on too long, comes from the fact that the world itself is not that reliable. Andy Warhol has predicted images will soon last "only twenty seconds". The reliable horse and buggy, the reliable bicycle, the reliable railroad train, the reliable DC-3, the reliably uncrowded international flights, the reliable French cuisine, the reliable foreign correspondent, have all been not totally eliminated, they are too reliable for that, but they have pushed into the peripheries of modern life.

The 3-1-2 strategy, beginning with a thorough consideration of

* Specifically the expansion of industry into the Urals and the opening up of Siberia that allowed the massive and extraordinary counterattack expansion that carried Soviet armies to the Elbe and the Danube.

Notes

desired purposes and results, then the appropriate thus-and-so to encounter with exact equilibrium the yes/no/somewhat of the given situation, makes the strategy of order, or of government (bureaucracy), enables the manager's monad to become clear and distinct.

"The minister of French education knows exactly what each student in France is studying at every minute." Voila! French culture, rational, "lux, calme, et volupteux", as Baudelaire wrote about its ideal. One problem: everyone else knows exactly what each student in France has studied. The German army studies the French plans and strikes at exactly its weak point, crossing the Moselle, which the French texts say more-or-less defends itself.

The manager uses this strategy to deal with the piled-up consequences of expansion, the losses of concentration, the facelessness of efficiency, the outdated image; he orders his domain, he prepares it to where it again becomes fit for action. Carried on too long, he becomes McClellan with a splendid Union Army that is losing the war although not so many men because he can't bear the disorder of battle, while Lee keeps expanding the Confederacy right to the outskirts of Washington itself, he becomes the Post Office management of 1900 that admired its perfection in dealing with rain, snow, and sleet, but as the information revolution arrived, found it couldn't deal with the electronic planetary world. The order strategy carried on too long becomes corrupt. The only way to get anything new done is to "know your way around", "deal", because "anything can be negotiated", "not getting caught is all that matters", "form instead of substance", "manners instead of friendship". The strategy's results become ripe for penetration by 1-2-3 strategies whether from within or without.

The manager uses the strategy of freedom when something authentically new must be introduced. He looks at the possible purposes/ results, the yes/no/somewhat and then comes out with a thus-and-so not foreseen, only umbrellaed by the 3 and 2. He gets by with it! A miracle! Lee Felsenstein and gang create the personal computer. The world changes and as if by magic. Edison, Tesla and gang create electricity. Von Braun and gang create the rocket era. Oppenheimer and gang create the bomb. Margulis et. al open our eyes to the constructive power of the microbes.

Freedom cuts in every direction. Its strategy pushed too far results in destruction. The world's expansions and concentrations, efficiencies, images, and hierarchies shatter, fall in bits and humans go berserk. Hitler and gang create Nazism in the Weimar Republic which was free, free, free. This destruction incarnate hurled the German peoples into their disastrous and criminal immolations.

Billy Sol Estes and co-workers create fake apparatuses and sell them for fortunes till amid uproar from the bilked he is imprisoned. In 1929 dozens of freedom strategies carried too long resulted in dozens of

Notes

men jumping from Wall Street skyscraper windows.

The world of the triad, dynamic, ever-changing; the manager uses this world to structure his strategies, to review them, to change them, to observe and deal with the strategies of competing monads.

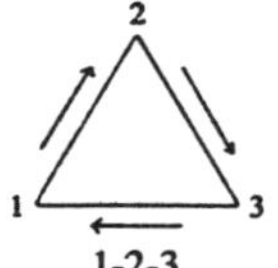

1-2-3

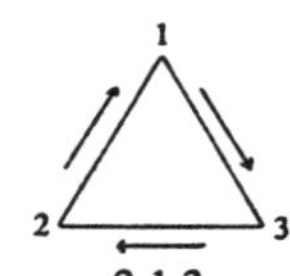

2-1-3

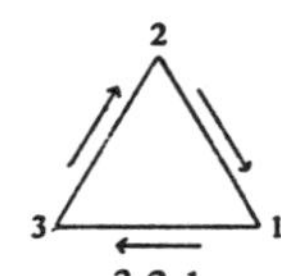

3-2-1

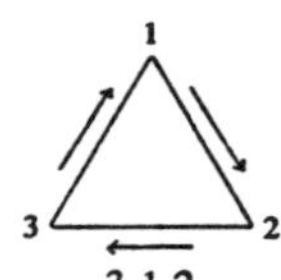

3-1-2

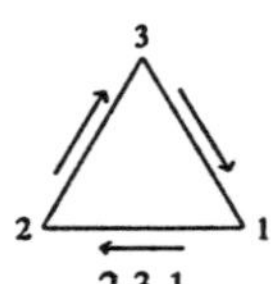

2-3-1

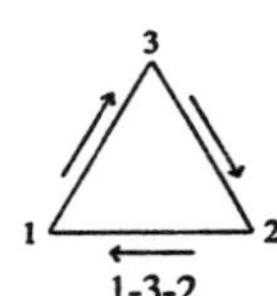

1-3-2

Try the exercise:

1) Pick the strategy that excites you the most in relation to your monad and dyads.
2) Draw the triangle and label the three points, thus-and-so, yes/no/somewhat, and purposes/results.
3) Using the numbers 1,2, and 3 as representations, number off in the order of the strategy you wish to explore.
4) Make the thus-and-so specific, for example, a 1-2-3: we will open up the $100,000,000 Desert Development Corporation in country X as a joint venture with the Government on Oct. 2 of the coming year. Go through the yes/no/somewhat of this thus-and-so. Pick out the "battles" that this will cause to be fought. Work out what you do when one of the battles is lost. Strategy is directed at winning a "war" not every "battle". Go over the range of results and purposes from "victory" to "win" to "draw" to "lose" to "catastrophe". Of course, you should use specifics from your actual monad, not an abstract example.
5) What strategy will you have ready to replace the 1-2-3 (expansion) if it becomes clear that its costs now exceed its benefits. How will that strategy extricate you from the various results of 1-2-3? Do you need more than one replacement strategy, that is, can such various consequences occur that more than one escape route is needed?
6) Contemplate your results.
7) Put the exercise aside until you feel that you would do this strategy if only you could be sure that your tactics are sufficient to carry it out. If they were, you would do it. If they weren't, you'd have to forget it. You aren't sure about it.
8) At this point move on to THE TETRAD.

The Triad

Notes

THE TETRAD

Notes

The manager has decided upon a strategy, let's say of expansion, to take best advantage of his monad's potentiality, using, say, the force of the dyad of risk/opportunity, to improve its relative standing vis-a-vis other monads, and to increase the richness of its inner content.

This strategy calls for a series of struggles: designing office A, laboratory B, factory C and then staffing A', B', C', then making productive A'', B'', C'', etc. The manager begins to wonder how he is going to do all of this.

At this point the manager should structure his thought to the demands of tactics. He draws a diagram of the tetrad.

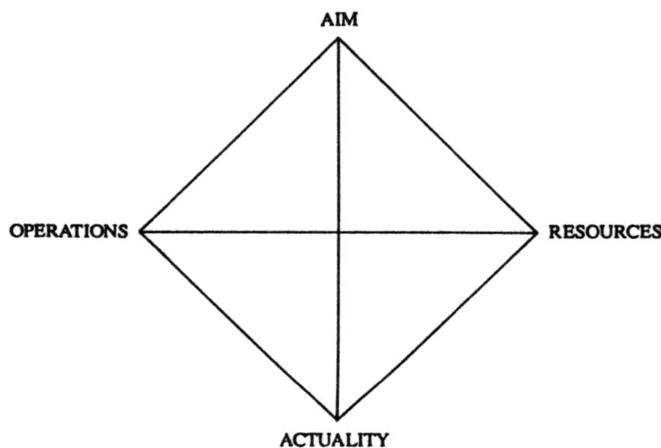

At the top he writes *goal* or *aim,* on the right side *resources,* on the left *operations,* and at the bottom point *actuality* and adds two connective lines.

We can see by inspection and also obtain by formula:

$$\frac{N^2 - N}{2}$$

that the tetrad possesses 6 dyadic connections.

The use of the tetrad falls into three stages: first, the manager determines the *aim,* (or why or what for) that he plans this expansion, then he investigates his *actuality,* what state-of-affairs prevails in his monad, internally and externally that must serve as the foundation to achieve this aim, then what are the *resources,* intellectual, characterological, financial, scientific-technical, etc. that he can call on to aid this venture from *actuality* to *aim,* and then he visualizes the *operation* necessary to carry out to bring the *resources* into play.

The discovery of the tetrad's power in antiquity, called earth *(actuality),* fire *(aim),* water *(operations),* and air *(resources),* exemplified in making the sundried brick called adobe in the American southwest, later conceptualized by Aristotle as the four causes that produce existential effects, final cause, theoretical cause, efficient cause, and formal cause, produced such exhiliration in ancient managers that this structure became deified in some cultures, such as the ancient Jewish, in which the sacred Tetragammetron, JHVH, became the hidden name of the Creator. And, indeed, he who masters the tetrad can make or create.

For the second step, the manager returns to the tetrad, and names the connective dyads for the quality of the intensity which they can be used to generate.

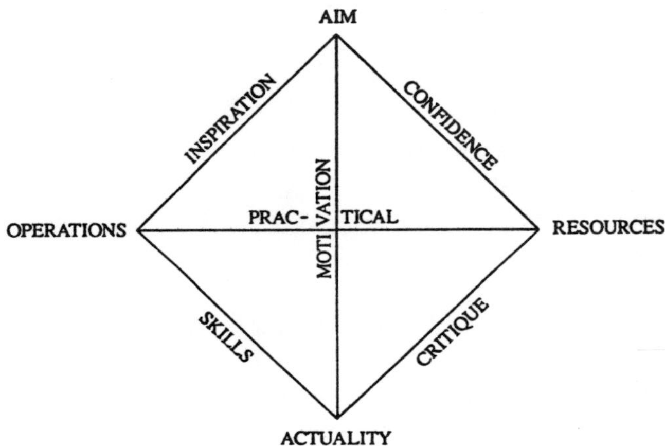

In using these connections, he brings the *aim* and *actuality* together in his attention, using the most vivid accurate formulations he can work up from contemplation of possibilities arising from engaging in the strategic "war", that is, victory or defeat, achievement or fortune. This effort will demonstrate to his experience the level of motivation contained within his tetrad. If the motivation does not reach dyadic intensity, then this casts great doubt on the viability of the strategy for the manager, as would the inability to reach such intensity with any of the other six dyads subordinate to the overall tetrad. A common failure here is for the manager to "aim for the *aim*", rather than to realize that *aim* and *actuality* are the poles of a dyad, that pure *aim* apart from pure *actuality* is not possible. An equal failure, of course, is the manager known contemptuously as the nit-picker, who endeavors to be "actual *actuality*", to get down to the "nitty-gritty", to "debunk those phonies who have their heads in the clouds". Pure actuality, of course, is equally impossible for a manager. The aim in these cases will always be found to be some version of maintaining the status quo.

Next the manager brings *resources* against *operations,* how

Notes

practical is the whole affair? It may be logical but is it logistical?

Operations research indicates the plant will work, but can it be financed and staffed? How intensely practical can he be?

Next he brings *resources* against *actuality,* is *actuality* in a state to receive reinforcements? Can *resources,* represented, let's say, by the World Bank officer, take the real facts from *actuality?* Can *actuality,* let's say represented by Prime Minister of X, take the International Monetary Fund's demand to change his country's investment patterns? Critique arrives. How intensely can the situation be critiqued before explosion arrives, how much can a sore point be left alone before freezing sets in?

The manager now turns to confronting *operations* and *actuality.* What skills are needed? What skills lacking? Which ones will emerge?

The manager brings *aim* and *operations* together. Will the ongoing operations inspire the leadership? Will the leadership inspire the operators? Do they realize that they are all in it together?

The question marks are not to be answered, they exist to raise intensity to the level of ability to perceive the true relationships, in this latter case of industrial expansion in country X. With these intensities the manager now sees that for his tetrad to support his strategy of expansion all its component triads must be 1-2-3. If he first takes the triad *aim-actuality-resources* he finds that: *aim* (thus-and-so) must act on *actuality* (yes-no-perhaps) and this will produce *resources* (results; see figure 1). Clearly if *actuality* comes before *aim* the *resources* would concentrate, or diminish (see fig. 2).

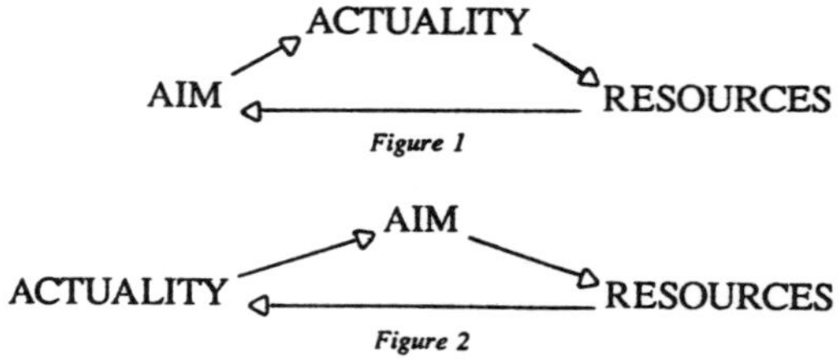

Figure 1

Figure 2

So the triad must be visualized *aim-actuality-resources* in order to align tactics with the previously chosen strategy of expansion.

The manager now checks out his remaining triads to move them to coordinate with the expansive strategy.

aim-actuality-operations,
operations-actuality-resources,
aim-operations-resources.

Good, we now have:

AIM	AIM	AIM	OPERATIONS
ACTUALITY	ACTUALITY	OPERATIONS	ACTUALITY
OPERATIONS	RESOURCES	RESOURCES	RESOURCES

Notes

Our affirmative power has *aim* in 3 triads plus one *operations*. We have *resources* as results in 3 triads plus one *operations*. We have increased *resources* and *operations,* and we have used *actuality* to the full together with one *operations* to produce the new surplus or expansion. *Aim* drives every triad that it can, and *operations* drives the other.

Tactics has been fully aligned with strategy. If, however, the manager finds that he cannot raise the six dyads to the intensity of distinct discomfort, of paradoxical or contradictory unity, or that his four triads refuse to accommodate themselves to the expansive modality, then he is well-warned to review carefully his monad, dyad, and strategy selected from the triads. An error exists either there or in the construction of his tetrad.

But once the tactics have been successfully worked out, and the strategy envisions a definite endpoint, Montgomery moves ever victoriously from El Alamein to Hamburg, Patton from Tunisia to Bavaria, Zhukov from Kursk to Berlin, MacArthur from Guadalcanal to Tokyo Bay, IBM crunches the Apple, the diner takes apart the lobster with immense enjoyment, the 13 Atlantic states expand to the Pacific in 59 years, Picasso produces the resume and program of painting, Japan, Inc. masters the export business, Russia takes over the revolution game, the eastern Mediterranean turns out religions, and the biosphere makes biomes.

The third step to make sure the tetrad works properly is to construct three circles or the center:

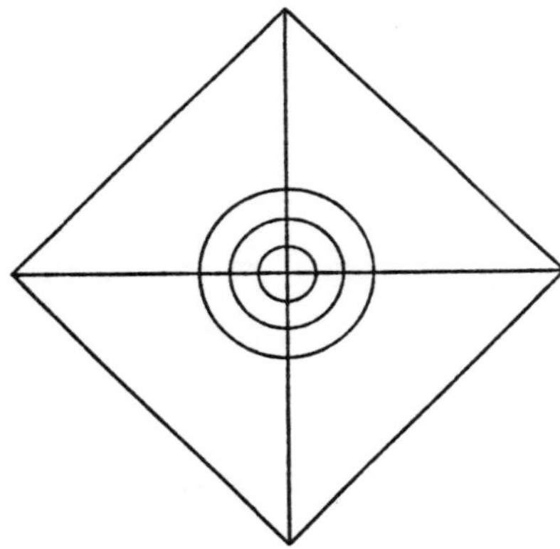

The first, smallest circle, represents the condition of trying to overcontrol the tetrad, to keep everthing "'tight".

Such are the "chicken-shit" lieutenants "fragged" by independent minded US E-2's and E-3's. America is continually reinforced by the "brain drain", creative individuals who leave or even flee tightly controlled state economies because they wish to produce their ideas otherwise ground down by meaningless vetoes and regulations. They wish to move their ideas into the hurly-burly of the great wide world for the big pay-offs, of which pay itself may be the smallest motive. The author personally has seen one major American corporation denuded of talent within a month of a "real crackdown on all those who didn't toe the new boss's line". One of those who left later had to be brought back naming his own conditions, of which, besides increased title and vastly increased emolument, a free hand in his area was predominant. A new corporate president had also been named.

The largest circle represents the "sloppy" outfit. The tetrad possesses an astonishing ability to survive rugged conditions in the field because of its "give", but too much "sloppiness", lack of communication between *resources* and *operations,* let's say, and the manager has "Humpty-Dumpty who had a great fall", and the pieces will never be picked up again; Guderian's tanks running out of gas twenty miles in front of the Kremlin, Paulus' cut-off army at the Volga, the collapse of the City Center all over America, Paris trembling in the balance with Les Halles *(resources)* removed, and the auto *(operations)* rampant over the Seine *(resources).* South Vietnam managers collapsed from a sloppy skewed circle pushing *aim* and *actuality* ever further apart, as indeed did Nicaraguan Somoza, the Argentine generals, and the Polish dictators.

The middle circle represents the rider on the horse relaxed but in control, reining but not viciously. He and his horse will go far over the prairie *(actuality),* pursuing his freedom *(aim),* watering, feeding, resting, grooming his horse *(operations),* with almost inexhaustible vitality *(resources).* So the director and his film, and any manager with his product.

Try the exercise:

(1) Take the strategy that you developed from the triad.
(2) Draw the tetrad and name the points and connection and draw the three circles at the center.
(3) Formulate *aim, actuality, resources,* and *operations* in words representing the real content of the real situation for which you have developed the strategy.
(4) Do the dyadic exercise on each of the six dyads unless the motivational one bores you, or the practical one infuriates you, or the confidence one dismays you, or the critique one makes you uptight, or the skills one makes you bewildered, or the inspirational one depresses you, in which case you start over again with new formulations, or even a new monad, if necessary. Not all monads can be developed past a triad. That is to say, they have been tested by structural thought and been found lacking in the ability to create their existential reality. In that case, the

Notes

exercise has sharpened your judgement, and prevented a disaster, because of course the test by existential forces is so much more costly than testing by thought.

For example, the German General Staff had been right all along about their being destroyed in an aggressive war, and Hitler wrong; he was a tactical lout, proved finally and absolutely on the Kursk Salient, and the success in France had been due to French betrayal not Hitler's tactics. Had they been structural thinkers they would have arrested him. German *resources* could not hold up this tetrad to carry out world expansion. Lyndon Johnson could find no *aim* in America that would produce a tactics for warlike American action in Southeast Asia. Fortunately, the American voters were able to dismiss him from the further sloppy conduct of their foreign affairs. The next president was dismissed by Congress for the sloppy handling of *operations* on internal affairs. Mr. Carter was retired in semi-disgrace for being too tight. So failure to reach a tetrad shows to the discerning manager, time to restructure his thought, before failing. Start over.

(5) With the six supportive dyads operative, bring the four supportive triads into coordination with your strategical triad. This can be called "all-out". It is possible to proceed under some conditions with three triads aligned and one supportive, say three 1-2-3's and one 1-3-2, but never contradictive say three 1-2-3's and one 2-1-3.

(6) Contemplate your results.

(7) Work on "the circles" until the whole tetrad "hums"' so smoothly, you say to yourself "I'm a genius" or something equally vapid, because immediately thereafter, if you have the stuff in you to go beyond field commander, forms in your attention the words "but so what?" or "what's all the shouting about?" It all appears "sound and fury signifying nothing" though you now understand how well it will work. But you realize you won't do it because it lacks sufficient meaning.

(8) At this point, move on to the PENTAD.

This is what Mr. Carter did not do when he organized his boycott of the Moscow Olympics, nor Mr. Reagan who organized his feud with Libya, nor Mr. Maxwell who took over *The Mirror,* nor any of the other managers who "made expense of spirit in a waste of shame".

Notes

THE PENTAD

Notes

Plato considered the dodecahedron with its twelve pentagonal faces to be the algorithm of perfected thought. The twelve because it showed the way to think about "all and everything", the pentagon because it showed that every key aspect, or "face", of reality had significance.

Significance occurs when the manager encounters choices demanding decisions needing sustained commitment to carry through. This kind of decisions occur when potentiality will be increased or decreased. To think about this requires that the manager deal with an entity, ent + ity= a whole being. The tetrad can deal with a process, but it does not matter who owns it, runs it, what its aim is. It can be bought and sold on a present-value basis and an extrapolated market. It is the limit of Harvard Business School's official thinking: "the bottom line". And Harvard Business School's thinking dominates the thinking of most managers today. Everything is judged by the present value rate of return on capital as evaluated by the keenest analysts. But dealing with increases of potentiality means considering "the top line"; how much are we able to do that we don't do but could do when we wish or need to? In a world full of clashing values, and sudden changes in fact (the fall of the Gang of Four and reversal of Chinese policy, or the mass introduction of the personal computer or the rise of the economy of the Pacific Basin), it seems clear that "dinosaurs" who have "bottom-lined" their product (developing the spine at the expense of the brain), and thus lost potentiality, will be swept aside upon conditions changing. With potentiality, significance cannot but saturate the art of the manager, because he must decide to do this and not that and that, or decide to build even more potentiality so that the significance of his decision will increase yet again. In short, the tetrad represents the forces of production and economics, but the pentad deals with entities and power. Hammer of Occidental, Land of Polaroid, and Crow of Trammel Crow are power, Texaco and Kodak marketing investments.

With the pentad the manager's choices become unique and therefore always interesting. Let us study the pentad closely:

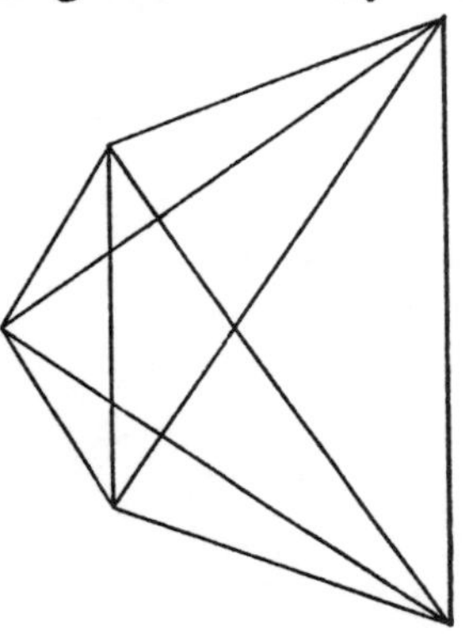

Notes

We see five points, of course, and note by inspection or formula that ten dyadic connections exist, seven triads, and five tetrads. Clearly we have reached a point of complexity where the author will no longer attempt to capture with linear word sequences this complex structure's totality. He will leave the dyadic work to the manager, and most of the triadic and tetradic work also, and concentrate upon the pentad proper. Since the manager possessing or possessed by authentic desire to think structurally has of course done the exercises up to this point, he will have mastered the requisite skills including the skill to use structural language.

An obligatory warning must be posted here, however, that no great harm although no good will have been done reading to this point without having thoroughly done the exercises. But after this point, one should remember most strongly that "concepts without percepts" are not only empty, but emptying, that is can "suck you dry". So true is this that only repeated requests by responsible managers to the author have caused the writing of this book, and then only after months of careful heart searching. The author suggests that the reader enclose this paragraph in a red line to make himself think about the formulation therein.

Let us put names on the five points of the pentad:

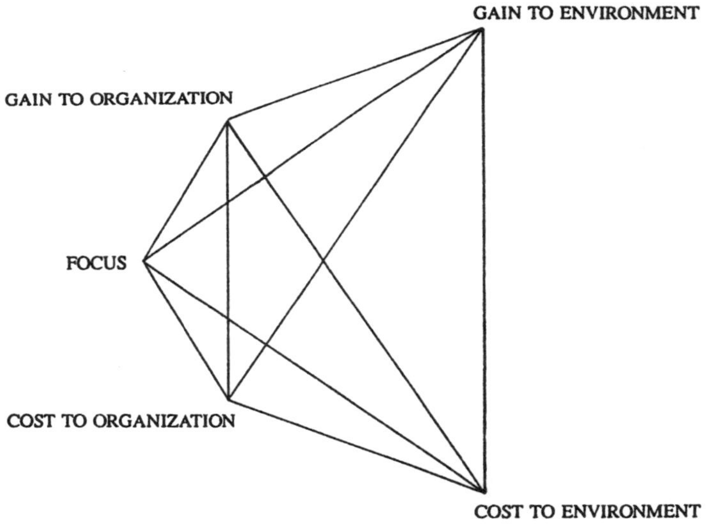

None of the previous structures enable the manager to focus all his capacity on a single point. To operate the pentad the manager must have a focus of such magnitude that all of his inner organizational concerns and outer organizational concerns concentrate on that point. IBM management focussed on information, not divided between computers and information. Humble focussed on energy not oil, gas, uranium, etc. Do you call up AT&T for information or telephones? How does AT&T decide? Well, probably difficultly, since they seem to have tried to keep two foci: telephones and information. Jefferson focussed on America "we are all Republicans, we are all Democrats". Lesser presidents caught in tetrads of highly productive insignificance say "we are Republicans and Americans" or similar difficult propositions with which to manage a great country. The present Pope is for religion and against birth control so the church is in a crisis of significance. Churchill said "I will ally with the devil himself (Stalin) against Hitler". No doubt of his focus. Or the fantastic significance of his choice.

Notes

Focus must be associated with pentadic structure or it becomes "tunnel vision", the "one-track mind", the man identified as a "fanatic". To insure that our focus can be properly adjusted to see whatever galaxy, star, planet, moon, or comet we wish, we need quite a complex telescope and it must be complete. Let's inspect once again the pentadic figure, this time numbering the points for ease of reference:

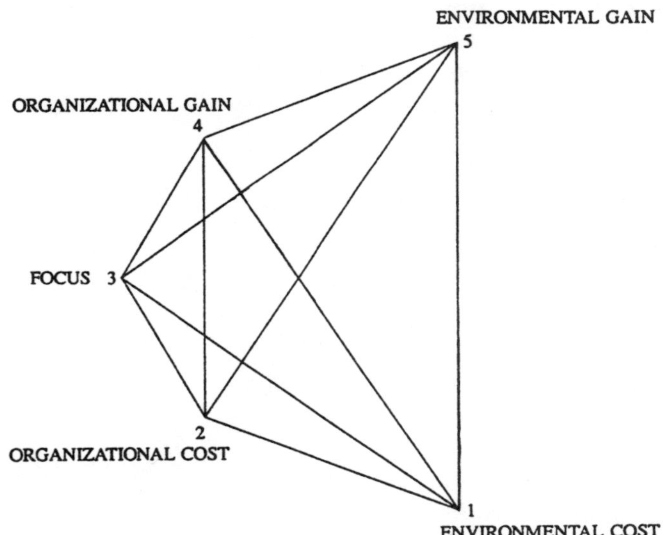

If the manager(s) focus the organization on something to the exclusion of the environment we get the silliness of Rajneeshpuram, the folly of the Edsel, the grim wreckage of the American Army in a country unknown, unstudied, and even unacknowledged. The pentad collapsed to the 2-3-4 points. A collapsed pentad can drive perfectly good tetrads to their doom. The American Army won its Vietnamese tactical set-pieces, a useless blood sacrifice to a management unaware of its environment. This was repeated in Iran and Lebanon and will be repeated again until the management decides to structure in the environment and what the environment will gain or lose by American actions. The Afrikaaner leaders have been taking their people down the same route since Apartheid was decreed in 1948, a deliberate collapsing of the Pentad to 2-3-4; the murders and defeat of Pol Pot of Cambodia further illustrate the grim horrors that can arise from making a god out of a focussed organization.

Notes

If the manager(s) focus the environment on their aim without a proper organization, you get a collapsed pentad of the 1-3-5 type which produces "world-figures" of the type of Nyerere of Tanzania, Nasser of Egypt, Nkrumah of Ghana, Peron of Argentina who drive their perfectly good nations to bankruptcy and sometimes defeat by never considering its gains and losses in their schemes to gain headlines on flaming issues of the day. Great industrial leaders like Howard Hughes decline into being prisoners of their house guard and their visions cease to have creative power. These examples illustrate the black comedy of what happens to an organization from making a god out of a focussed environment.

We do see two key triads in the pentad, points 1-3-5, and points 2-3-4, which of course, tell us that we need two key strategies, one for the organization on its inner side, and one for the organization on its outer side, but they both must have exactly the same focus to avoid the consequences alluded to above.

The focus of the American enterprise has been, from its inception, inalienable rights, and when managed properly at the pentadic level has had a domestic policy and a foreign policy which, widely divergent because of the divergence between conditions internal and external to America, have nonetheless focussed on the same point. Kennedy's photos were seen in places of mourning all over America, but also in Asian and African streets and European plazas. With both Roosevelts, Lincoln, Jefferson, and Washington, this same power was evoked. It lies latent in the Presidency for anyone capable of seeing it, unless of course the entity should lose its significance due to a long series of bad managers.

Point 1, the cost to the environment is, in ecological terms, "what the focus eats", and point 5, is "who eats the focus", or what does the environment gain? The mining industry could see little gain in Bunker Hunt's speculative mode of approach dominating silver and so they wiped him out. The people thought thalidomide cost too much deformity for its gains and they regulated further the pharmaceutical industry. Points 1 and 5 make the entity's econiche in the external world. The American "constituency" has been those "yearning to be free", free, that is of existential alienations of their essentially inalienable rights (among them, life, liberty, and the pursuit of happiness), and the cost to the environment has been the loss of these people to America. Berlin Walls and various other barriers have been instituted by states who don't wish to pay this cost because they have so far seen little gain for themselves in assisting the existence of America.

There does not exist, then, an "American people" like the "French people" or the "Russian people". Everyone yearning to be free in the

Notes

world assists Jeffersonian America, the focus "eats", grows strong by, every elimination of an abridgement to these essentially inalienable, but all too often existentially taken away rights. Literally, millions of those yearning to be free come to America to work for this focus, other millions work for alliances, trade, intellectual, musical, dance, theatrical, scientific, financial consulting, fashion exchange in order to "get a little". The "reservoir of good will" that Wendell Willkie found for America around the world and which still exists is for this pentadic America.

Who "eats" these inalienable rights are all those who have become to some degree free in in disposing of their life, arranging their liberty, pursuing their happiness. America gives great opportunities to the free to enjoy their freedom, though that may only be to ship their goods to the American market, or to buy uncensored opinion, or to dream of escape.

Those who "yearn to be free" must assist in the attainment of inalienable rights. Those who "are free" live off the "inalienable rights" and must demonstrate by the fruit that the tree is good if the pentad is to work. To some degree the Democratic Party gives a mode to insure point 1 is kept in view, the Republican Party point 5. Unfortunately, neither party has much use for culture or the intelligentsia, and therefore France, Italy, and England earn much of their living by supplying these inalienable rights to artists who by and large are excluded from the American mainstream although Manhattan has made it its particular vocation to do this within the U.S.

The people inside America must, however, on the lower inside limit, be assured of existential security, economic welfare, housing, an interesting daily life. If not, Know-Nothing and racist movements arise perceiving a threat to their own enjoyment of "inalienable rights" by the manager "giving too much away", "being too concerned with foreigners", that is, or it costing them too much.

On the gains of the organization, the American people must, on the whole, perceive life getting better, their understanding developing, that their open road has not been herded into a suburban mall's dead end to die in a carcinogenic haze, that a man or a woman is still "able to go to hell in his own way", that "going to Mars is possible, or even the stars", that enlightenment can still strike on Washington Square or in the Wind River Range. If this is not satisfied, the "revolt of the leaders" will occur, and they expatriate to overseas development, or disappear into the interstices of the North American continent as prospectors, hobos, mountain men, and desert rats.

Whatever entity the manager thinks about requires that he consider these five points, making the same focus for two separate triads, one dealing with those inside his organization for their maintenance and development and one for dealing with those in the world outside his

Notes

organization in the case of a business those who form their suppliers and those who form their users.*

The manager should remember that the pentadic structuring effort is only possible for the man who has mastered the tetrad, is fully productive, who subsists existence, and then wishes to secure significance for himself, not a sterile success that will be either left by himself in a short time, mocked by his family, sold out by his shareholders, or abandoned by society. The fates of Howard Hughes severed from TWA, Steven Job from Apple, Jerry Brown of California from elective office show what happens to managers who wish for more but can't provide a focus for their entity's outer connections.

If a pentad does become established, it may still deteriorate unless the tetrads 2-3-4-5, and 1-2-3-4 are brought into balance. In the 2-3-4-5 case, the 2 that is the organization itself works to become transformed into the benefits for the gain of the environment. If this tetrad dominates, the organization becomes bitter, "we're being exploited", "it's us they're making the killing off of". The disillusionment of many of the 1960's communal idealistic enterprises, and the bitter strikes in certain industries show these results. If the 1-2-3-4 tetrad dominates, the environment (nature, creditors, suppliers, immigrants) are the base, and the power and glory and creativity of the organizational members is the aim. This enterprise then becomes perceived as "living off the fat of the land", "riding high-and-mighty", inventories and properties pile up, use declines, and the environment forecloses by revolution, litigation, terror, theft, expropriation, or contempt. The case of the Polish Party and the Gang of Four in China are classic cases of the 1-2-3-4 taking over, the gains of the organization becoming so great that the environment revolted, and Stalin's apparatchik overthrow of Trotsky's world revolution a classic case where the organization felt exploited for the sake of foreigners they felt were living off their efforts. Trotsky had ignored the cost to Russia of his fantastic schemes, and the ordinary party member backed Stalin's revolt which then moved down to a 1-2-3-4, for the sake of the organization collapsed pentad. Clearly these two tetrads show that benefits must be spread between the organization

*The equation of suppliers with sellers and users with buyers generates most of the difficulties for business, whether capitalist or socialist. The community(ies) and nature also supply and use. The fact that this has been largely unaccounted till now reflects only that human societies still exist basically in a hunting-gathering-nomadic ("flight of factories") mode, and are designed (explicitly in mining and oil) for a limited number of years exploitation. With the effective closure, populating, and industrializing of the planet, these as yet unaccounted costs and benefits become ever more obvious. Unfortunately many reform movements count only 1-2-3-4, and while they are eloquent on the costs to the environment of an entity do not show where point 5, gains, are or can be made. Mobil Oil illustrates the classic opposite bent in its endless advertisements which basically stress 2-3-4-5 and do not mention the costs which destroy its credibility.

Notes

and the users. Nonetheless, the above examples are tetrads of collapsed pentads, not ordinary productive balanced tetrads, because everyone at each "beat" of the process felt the loss of world-historic significance involved. In the tetrad as an end in itself, no one feels the sense of loss, of "might-have-been", only "not enough" or "meaninglessness".

Understanding the pentad marks the first step of the manager's attainment of subtlety and the creative ability to lead. Thus George Marshall, with Roosevelt's concurrence, coordinated the European and Pacific Wars, and later coordinated the economic recovery of the states of Western Europe. Military tacticians like Patton, MacArthur, Eisenhower, Bradley, Nimitz, were given the fullest scope to produce. Later he gave the same scope to Monnet, Schumann, and Hoffman, the economic tacticians. Understanding the significance of each decision marks the first step toward "greatness". The manager must educate himself into taking account of variables changing in both the actualizing, "visible" world, and the non-actualizing, "invisible", potential world, that so much mightier world in which the way is difficult to find, and difficult to follow, and any "blinking" loses the focus, any greed for results endangers the impartial balancing of gains and costs for the environment, and vanity and pride threaten the esprit de corps of the organization.

Try the exercise:

1) Take the tetrad that you developed. See if you can find a focus for all that productivity. If you can't, then you must start over with the monad that contains the seed of a pentad. Not all monads contain significance when fully developed.
2) Draw the pentad, number the points, and label.
3) Make specific names for each of the five points of your environment.
4) See whether the focus of the organization is indeed also the focus for dealing with the environment. Check the connections. Is each charged with intensity? Are the two key triads on the same strategy? Are the two key tetrads in balanced operation? How much further can you sharpen your sensation that all of this focusses to a point? That you can commit the vectors of organization, essential and existential, and environment, suppliers and users, into a single decision concerning the change of its potential and the concomitant commitments.
5) What new attention must be paid to balance up the four other points of the pentad after this key decision has been made? That is, what changes will have to occur in the existing organization and in the existing environment?
6) Contemplate your results.

Notes

7) Don't move past this exercise till you begin to feel eager to apply this focussed potentiality -- be it information, or energy, or the new*, or victory** -- at a specific time/place/people intersection. Significance is no longer adequate. You wish to do it right there and then with so-and-so and with such-and-such skills. You wish to make an event, a legend, to transcend the entropic threats of time itself.
8) At this point move on to THE HEXAD.

* Baudelaire decided to make the *new* ("toujours le nouveau") the focus of all his artistic enterprise, thus giving rise in the hands of those who have understood to the now over-a-century-long succeed of the Avant-garde.

** Galileo decided to make *victory* (of knowledge over ignorance) the focus of his scientific enterprise, thus giving rise in the hands of those who have understood to the now over-three-centuries-long succeed of science which continually announces new victories (over disease, over causes of pollution, over space, over time, over matter, over energy, over language, over the gene, and over ever-new-encountered ignorances.)

Notes

THE HEXAD

Notes

IBM does something significant, unquestionably -- information. But where's the legend, the glamour, the immortal place in history, the event? Would anyone be able to locate IBM if AT&T or the Japanese did knock it out of the market? But Ford started the mass production/ consumption era in Detroit in 1905 with all the workmen who showed up for the top dollar offer of the day. Ford presidents go forth to run World Banks or save Chrysler. Ford himself was lauded by Stalin as the man who knew the way to produce the abundant life for Russia and made a god by Huxley in his novel, *Brave New World.* Ford is immortal within the limits certainly of the history of western technical civilization.

On a November afternoon in 1924 Knute Rockne's Four Horsemen rode triumphantly over Army with beauty and precision and Notre Dame began the American football legend. Doubtless the evolutions of Oklahoma, Texas, and Alabama football are significant for football, but Knute Rockne's mathematics of the shift and the passion of the half-time speech, the creation of a "team" marked the event from which American football draws endless strength. By playing on the movie screen Knute Rockne's most famous player, the Gipper, Ronald Reagan garnered the glory from the aura of this event, and has known how to use it all the way.

On November 7, 1917, Lenin ordered the arrest of Kerensky's ministers sitting in the Winter Palace in the city of Petrograd and declared a new government. On the Eighteenth of Brumaire, 1798, Napoleon Bonaparte seized the power of the French Revolution in Paris.

The remembered dullness of who, what, when, and where, due to the poor imitation of education that has taken over the world's classrooms must not keep the manager structuring his thought from realizing that the names, dates, and locations in history represent the fiery complexity where *significance* advanced into the structure of an *event* which has the property of *recurrence,* or the ableness-to-be-itself throughout vast changes of time. They are clues that beckon students of reality.

Let us look at a structure:

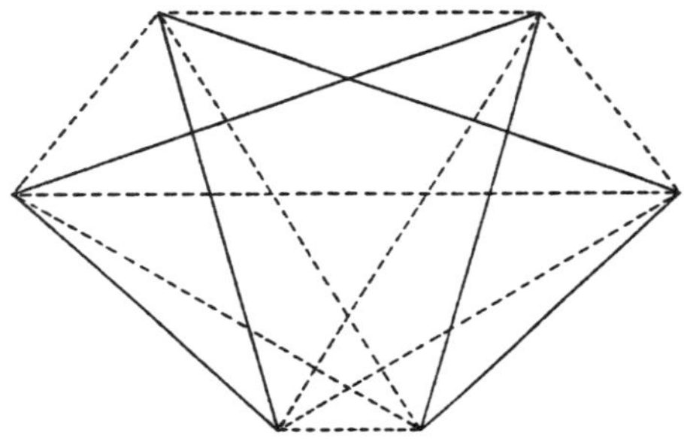

Notes

Inspection or formula gives us twelve connective dyads but to begin we will not deal with the ones represented by dotted lines. We will use only:

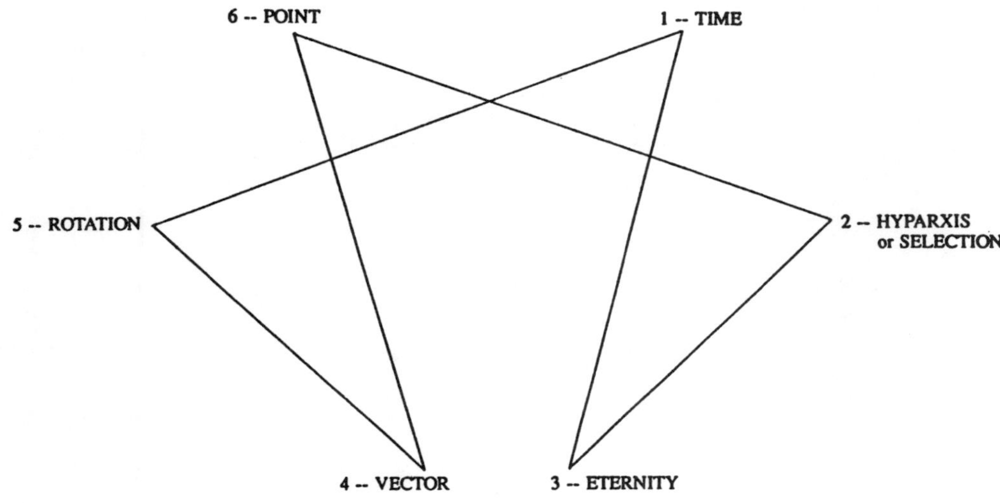

Point one represents *time,* the successive perception of the situation by the senses if they were not interrupted by memory or imagination. *time* as represented by the ever-moving sand, or shadow, or hour and minute hands, or digits.

Point three represents *eternity,* the cornicopia of potentialities really inherent in the situation.

Point two represents *selection,* the ableness-to-choose the potentiality which sets off the next set of actualizations.

Point six represents *positional space,* the "point" (which might be a Notre Dame Stadium, the Winter Palace, the Ford Motor Company at Dearborn).

Point four represents *vectorial space,* the key directions that play upon the "point". 1917-1918: Berlin, Paris, London, Tokyo, Washington are cathexed toward Petrograd; troops, ships, money begin to move along fields of force. Petrograd becoming Leningrad is cathexed toward Moscow, Murmansk, Vladivostok, Tsaritsyn, Kiev; ideas, troops, institutions begin to move along fields of force.

Point five represents *rotational space,* represented by latitude, longitude, elevation, season, year, period, epoch, era, and eon.

With these six great dimensions, the manager structures his event. Leary, Ginsberg, et. al. decide that "The Human Be-In" will occur on January 1 in Golden Gate Park in San Francisco in 1967. And the forces must be set in motion so that all arrives at this concentration that's necessary to make an *event,* the stuff of myth, legend, history.

Notes

Napoleon chooses the battleground of Austerlitz (position), foresees the movements (vectors and rotations) of his antagonists, selects the decisive moment, and then orders his elite forward into the breach of the Allied Armies and becomes Emperor.

Clive at Plassey destroys the army of the Moguls, and the British Empire begins its two centuries reign.

Nothing can be undone at these moments; choice, decision, commitments have been brought together and significance becomes real. "The event", said Washington "is in the hands of God", but only "after setting a standard to which the wise and honest may repair", that is, a pentad.

Michelangelo chooses a "ruined" block of marble to make good his claim to sovereignty; from that cracked block emerges "David", the young Renaissance destroys the Goliath of Medieval allegory.

By inspection, we see that there must be six pentads, or six significances to make a hexad:

```
1 2 3 4 5
1   3 4 5 6
1 2   4 5 6
1 2 3   5 6
1 2 3 4   6
  2 3 4 5 6
```

Let us take the pentad with 1-3-4-5-6: the manager must then select from the 2, the move(s) that will fix once-and-for-all the *event* after which nothing-will-be-the-same-again. Kyoto is proposed for the first atomic bomb, Stimson remembers Kyoto because of all the varied *events* that have made it sacred and therefore to be spared (as also were Paris and Rome in the West), and so the industrial city Hiroshima becomes the position for the atomic *event*. Stimson was "hyparchically" there. He saw the six significances flashing. He had first opposed Imperial Expansion in 1930 as Secretary of War for Hoover in Manchuria. Fifteen years later, Secretary for War for Roosevelt and then Truman, he had structured an understanding of the situation. Could he have chosen better?

Let us take the pentad 2-3-4-5-6. Now the manager must decide the time of the event. Truman says "As soon as possible". Could he have chosen better? With the event, the manager will never know. "The die is cast". "Caesar crosses the Rubicon". There is no turning back now. Pompey and the Senate will fight. "Atom Bomb Dropped on Hiroshima." The world knows we have entered the atomic era. Russia, Britain, France, China and who knows whom will build them.

The Hexad

Notes

Lyndon Johnson orders "escalation" in Vietnam. Ho Chi Minh orders "counter-escalation". America writhes, trapped in an undeclared war.

American auto executives decide small gas-economical cars have no commercial future in the United States. Detroit loses the leadership in the world auto industry.

These sentences conceal the complex structure of an *event*. For the U.S. actually to commit aggression on the territory of North Vietnam as distinct from defending South Vietnamese territory, the bombing, which produced the *event* of the first great failure of U.S. foreign policy, required long years of preparation by the China lobby, the Air Force, the Texas oilmen, the South Vietnamese military, the North Vietnamese party. The groundwork was carefully laid including the legal basis: the rushed through Tonkin Gulf Resolution. An *event* can be thoroughly structured but that is no guarantee of how the *event* will turn out as its structurers hope, for with so many entities's significance at stake, a struggle with unpredictable outcome is sure to ensue, the very struggle whose energies make the hexad achieve such a real being in potentiality as well as in actuality that its meanings can recur for perhaps as long as human history, until all its possibilities are realized.

The French Revolution for example: in one episode Robespierre cut off Danton's head with the aid of Saint Just, but lost his own thereafter. Stalin, identifying himself as Robespierre, exiled Trotsky, his Saint Just, then killed Bukharin, his Danton, and won. Mao (Robespierre) and Chou En-lai (Danton) played to a stand-off, the Gang of Four (Saint Just) swept to power but Deng, Chou's successor (Danton), with Robespierre naturally dead, jailed but did not kill the Gang of Four. Castro (Robespierre) jailed Mateos (Danton) and sent Che Guevara (Saint Just) off to be killed in Bolivia. But one can see that all this is recurrence of the French Revolution each time coming out a little differently because of the unpredictablility of the details of the struggle. And each new recurrence adds to the realization of the possibilities hidden in July 14, 1789, at the storming of the Bastille.

Managers who have become capable of structuring events realize how precarious and brief their moment of decision is, "how much hangs in the balance". They study related events closely. *Plutarch's Lives* which give accounts of Roman and Greeks who operated on at least this level, have been read by managers for nearly two millennia.*

Study Plutarch's account of Caesar crossing the Rubicon, of Solon instituting the Athenian state, Alcibiades destroying the Athenian empire, Numa commencing Rome on its long career of ruling by religious superstition. Reflect upon *Plutarch's Lives*. Was it itself an

*The man who set the Mexican Revolution decisively on course was actually named Plutarco Calles.

Notes

event?

Plato decides to found the Academy from which all our universities spring, instead of striking for the rulership of Athens which he evaluates as "washed-up"; Aristotle leaves Athens a generation later and joins the Macedonians to give Alexander the intellectual basis to create the Hellenistic era instead of remaining a Yale to Plato's Harvard.

To understand these, work your way through the connections, the intensity between time and eternity, time and position, time and vector, time and rotation, time and selections, eternity and selection, eternity and position, eternity and direction, eternity and rotation, selection and position, selection and direction, selection and rotation, position and direction, position and rotation, direction and rotation, then decide upon a strategy and proceed to arrange the triads to co-ordinate, then arrange the tetrads to produce, and focus the six pentads.

Then you will see the beauty, say, of Gandhi's march to the sea for salt. Remember he at that moment could have selected from nearly countless alternatives to make the event to begin the road to independence.

The rightness of the decision to put the first great electric plant at Niagara Falls and with alternating current. The power of von Braun joining the Americans. The stepping into the unknown of Hofmann's revealing the properties of LSD-25. They had structured the situation, their decision locked dimensions into myth, into legend, into raw material for history, for reality.

Try the exercise:

(1) Draw the hexad and write down the formal names.
(2) Substitute actual time, position etc. of the situation you are structuring.
(3) See if you can find a range of key decisions in the hexad you are working on. The range will be determined by the choices available in the potentialities of the pentads. God help the company reduced to a tetradic cash flow-junk bond payout operation by the corporate raiders and conventional HBS analysts. Such companies, and therefore their managers, are eliminated from participating as principals in events, in other words they are powerless participants whose actions can be calculated in advance by event managers.
(4) Work for the top decision alternatives for your projected effects on each of the six pentads.
(5) What about the differing viewpoints of the various pentads? Can you structure them in as Caesar and Gandhi did, but as Johnson failed to do with Ho Chi Minh, the Air Force, the Media, the Army, the S. Vietnamese, and the Montagnards, as Reagan and Haig failed to do in

okaying the Israeli advance into Lebanon? If you can't, then you are approaching an event, but a legendary disaster event, within the limits of your fortuitous capacity to meddle.

(6) Contemplate your results.

(7) Don't move past this exercise till you wish to structure this raw material of history into history, into transforming the event into something completely different than itself, and thereby transcending fate to arrive at destiny, a connection to all events throughout all the dimensions of existence.

(8) At this point move on to THE HEPTAD.

Notes

Notes

THE HEPTAD

Notes

The event guarantees its existential status as a reality that can for long overcome entropy by having six dimensional coordinates. The fifth dimension of potentiality, "the storehouse of possibilities", and the sixth dimension of selection, "ableness to choose", guarantee for some shorter or greater four-dimensional period of actualization the recurrence of the event, though the actuality will be differently aspected with each new selection. After realization of all its possibilities it will remain contactable so long as traces of it remain. These traces of events can be found in what are call traditions. The genuine world-traveller is the one who journeys to various events by the contacting of tradition in the various localities travelled to, or museums visited, or people talked to, or symbols crafted exactly as once upon a time. But the event does not enter world history until it can transform itself and enter the "war of values" as a creative element.

To transform means that (1) the event must fully realize itself, (2) the event must become integrated into a greater world, and thereby, (3) the event and the greater world must both be irreversibly changed.

The event must fully realize itself because if it has not achieved its form, it cannot transform.

The event must be integrated into a greater whole, the world of history, because without other forms to draw energy from, it could not have the energy to go beyond itself and then sooner or later will be destroyed as its stock of possibilities is exhausted and their traces in actualization obliterated. This could take geologic eras, of course.

The event and the greater world must both be changed together otherwise the apparent transformation would be reversible back to being an event. Real time must pass to make it irreversible, and this flow of real time, evolution, a line of transformations, requires sacrifice, in this case sacrifice of the event's self-sufficiency.

Both the managers of the American Revolution and the Russian Revolution brandish threats that the other's revolution can be turned back out of history into an event. But in reality neither of the set of managers has been ready, willing, or able to allow their event and the greater world to change together irreversibly. So both revolutions at the bottom are anxious about their place in history, and rightly so. The agricultural and industrial revolutions, have, however "made their seven", transformed into history, and be it Moscow, Washington, Delhi, or Quito, everyone lives in that history. But, neither Washington nor Moscow will as yet allow their event to be irreversibly changed by the greater world. The first one that does so will change world history because the greater world will also be changed by that occurrence.

The Heptad

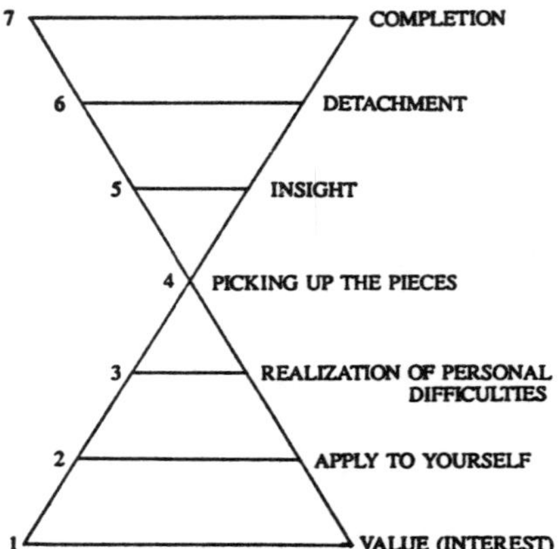

Notes

The heptad commences with *value.* We cannot perceive nor conceive value directly, but we can perceive interest directly and once we know the key equation relating quantity and quality: I=f(V), interest is a function of value, we can say that without intense interest a manager can never begin to structure a transformation. A great manager is never afflicted by boredom.

Science is a heptad that has transformed an event and the "great world". Galileo, the man who transformed the event of his discoveries and the "great world" by writing brilliantly about them, their supporters and their opponents, then disseminated this writing to the educated world, attained to poetry by interest in observation, measurement, hypothesis, experiment, technique, instrumentation, and description, so highly did he value exact knowledge. Now no one can edit science out of history because without science no manager would last. Stalin with all his power had to reinstate Einstein and Mendel (relativity and genetics) or his world would have disappeared from relevance as did Hitler's which eliminated economics and anthropology.

The second step in the heptad's seven steps is *applying that interest to yourself.* Galileo put himself on the line. He confronted himself confronting the world with his new interest, the world of quantities without any other quality except the ineluctable quality of quantity, exactness, accuracy, non-concealment.

The third step, *the realization of personal difficulties* in structuring the transformation. After all, love of the form, interest in the form begins the route to trans-form. Oscar Wilde put it "Each man kills the thing he loves"... by transforming it "up or down". The personal difficulty is "to let go". Galileo loved his music, his wine, his Firenze, and that brought him back from the free industrially progressive city of Venice to the papal dominated economically stagnant Firenze, into the hands of authoritarians whose power base was a combination of ignorance and belief and backwardness. His emotions, his sensations loved that which his will and intellect forged the instruments to surpass.

The fourth step, *picking up the pieces* after the shattering

Notes

realization. Galileo picks up all the pieces of his intellectual life, the intellectual life of the common man, the intellectual life of the era, Copernicus, Kepler, the intellectual opposition of the dogmatists, for the raw material for his book.

Then, the fifth step coming after his exhaustive survey of the pieces, *insight,* he "sees into" the way to present his beloved science, reaches the sixth step, *detachment,* necessary to go through his hearing in front of the inquisitional threats, and the seventh step, *completes* his mission by smuggling out his manuscripts to the greater world of Holland which is intellectually close to that of Great Britain and there, in the crucibles of the free discussions of the Royal Society, his science is changed to a higher state by Newton et.al., the world is changed, transformation occurs, the transformation that had eluded the great Egyptian, Chaldean, Greek, Roman, and Chinese scientists so that their steam engines, rockets, mathematics remained at best events, more often significant exceptions, in the course of world history. After Galileo's extraordinary management, "things would never be the same again", science and the great world were in irreversible connection, and both had grown in stature.

The symbol of the structure of seven shows several important aspects. *Picking up the pieces* is shown to be the central activity in structuring the heptad. Shock after shock will occur as beginning formulation, organization, logistics break down. Murphy's Laws admirably sum up the difficulties in the way of one attempting a transformation:

> (1) If it is impossible for anything to go wrong, something will go wrong.
> (2) If anything goes wrong, everything will go wrong.

Only Finagle's Factor can deal with this situation, and therefore point 4 represents this factor *picking up the pieces*. Great subtlety, resourcefulness, and patience are required for Finagle's Factor to appear.

The *interest* (point 1), must be broad-based for it must carry the load of the other 6 levels. The *completion* can only be as broad as the *interest* that began to structure the transformation.

The seven levels must be looked at in three ways: as successive steps in time, present all at once, and each demanding concentrated effort to analyze as if central to the entire effort, and this analysis will produce a small heptad "inside" each step of the large heptad.

For example: take step one, *value*. The manager must value *value,* or become interested in his *interest*. He can no longer take his *interest/ values* for granted. He must concentrate interest on the heptad.

Then he must *apply value to himself*. Does he properly value

Notes

himself? He must end self-deprecating and assess himself realistically, become interested in this assessment. English or French managers often end here by becoming "amused" rather than interested in self-assessment.

Then does he value *realizing his personal difficulties?* Then is he interested in *picking up the pieces?* Or is it only an irksome duty?

Then is he interested in *insights?* in *detachment?* in *completion?* Then realizing how valuable his valuing is, can he now let go of his interest so that it merges with the greater world, in this case, his original heptad, so that, irreversibly, the first step and the whole transformation process are now changed?

To make transformation requires an immense thought investment.

Even when a manager decides to go all-out plus his dreams, to structure a transformation is almost impossible because of the following facts:

If a manager commences with interest at A and desires to end with transformation B, so that

he then constates that time must elapse between A and B so that the world in which he began A is no longer that same world by the time B would be reached. And since the world is uncertain and relative, as well as being vast and quick, he cannot calculate the logistics, moral and physical, needed at A to overcome the obstacles in the way to B. Nonetheless he must so calculate in order to begin, adding of course his 10% contingency. Still the situation will look like this after a while:

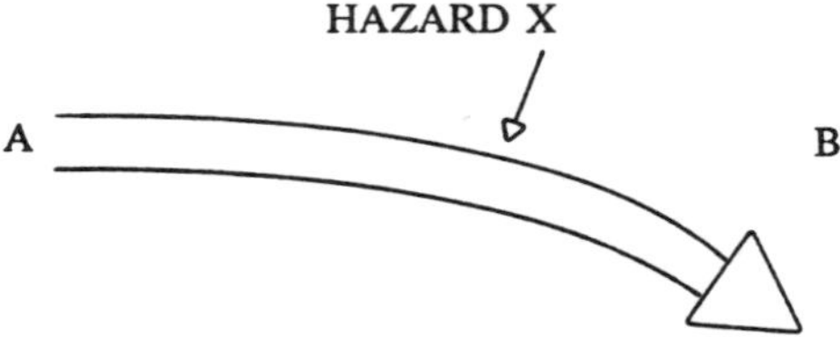

If another force, C does not come to the assistance of the manager's line, A, like so:

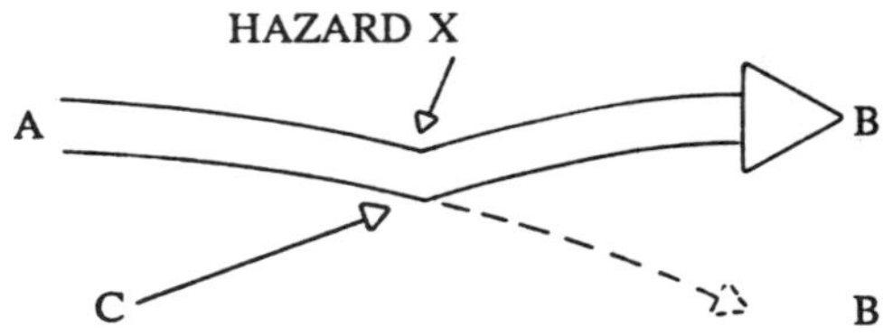

then it is clear that A will not reach B, form will not transform.

Notes

The manager must so structure his heptad, that at its third point, *realization of personal difficulties,* he opens himself up to an external shock from some other heptad (transformational effort) for that extra force he needs. First difficulty, not that many heptads are operating; second difficulty, only some of the operating heptads go in somewhat the same direction. A sharp lookout and appraisal plus luck give one a chance.

Washington must welcome Paine, Lafayette, and the people-rousing pamphlets of the French Enlightenment to his revolution of the unjustly taxed property owners or the transformation of colonies to nation will not be made.

Another difficulty now arises:

The interest to bring A---B suffices only to bring together all the powers inherent in A. (A + C)'s shock will reach B, but the value at B now does not suffice to pay for the extra and unpredicted effort required. Unless a *higher value* (greater interest) discovers itself, the success of the heptad transformation will lead to the greatest tragedy of all, the disillusionment with transformation, explored very well in King Lear, most recently in Kurosawa's movie version, *Ran.*

The new value D has to increase the value of B to higher value B'' in order that B'' becomes a satisfying structure for the effort put into the heptad. Otherwise the effort becomes a failed heptad, and no new transformation will be undertaken, "it costs too much", and the manager, although apparently succeeding, will only have suffered success from which point he will be cast down by his own disillusionment, that is, for him, B will seem only an illusion, not reality, and for him that will be the truth.

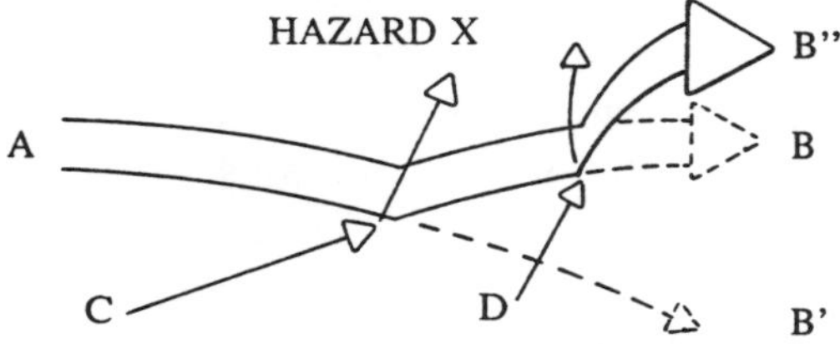

Note that after C gives the shock to A, C continues on its own way thereafter, as does D after its shock.

Washington and Lafayette receive the sword of Cornwallis but the gigantic effort required to overcome the crown has raised expectation so high that now no one is satisfied with the first heptad's accomplishment of Jefferson's Declaration of Independence. Jefferson must add new value to the revolution by including the First Ten Amendments to the Constitution originally proposed by the Convention, of which Washington was president for the new nation. These Ten Amendments from D began moving the B of American

Independence to a *higher value,* B'', not only a free nation for property but a just nation for the people. That B'' was not to be achieved until after the Civil War, the New Deal, and the Civil Rights Movement. Unfortunately, no leader has emerged to begin accomplishment of the new octave although perhaps in the Environmental Protection Act lie the seeds. The sense of stopping in the midst of success, unequalled in the world, instead of moving on to succeed, threatens America as nothing before in its history. A true manager would begin to move the essentially completed* free and just heptad toward a new objective. Perhaps the Environmental Protection movement's extension toward identifying sources not only of pollution and chemical problems but also of potential profits, asthetics, and national security in developing new energy sources, energy efficiencies, and recycled material use, could be the A for this second heptad as national freedom was the A for the first American heptad. And down the road one can envision space exploration becoming the C of the second octave. America the free, the just, the ecological, the cosmic. This would be *succeed* on quite a grand scale in grand style.

Heptads can be of different magnitudes or scales.

Earlier in this section it was stated that neither the American nor Russian Revolution had finished the transformational step; neither was fully integrated into the world order, and neither they nor the world order had become irrevocably changed. So in the American national political transformations that we are now speaking of, as differentiated from the American revolutionary idea per se, the American nation represents the greater world of local political movements, freedom, justice, environmental protection. But for the American Revolution its greater world is the planet Earth and although that revolution has made an event out of its life, liberty, and the pursuit of happiness, and the other inalienable human rights, that revolution has not reached integration with the world nor has the greater world fully accepted it and the changes that would involve in the greater world. The American Revolution remains American as the Russian Revolution remains Russian. Could the Soviet political appeal to the economically oppressed world be the C shock that added to the American Revolution world complete its heptad? And could the values of the ancient cultures of the world be the D shock, the addition of values that could make the whole process so satisfactory as to launch humanity into the next great succeed, biospheric cultures into space? Another alternative would be a Soviet leader using the American appeal to inalienable rights as the C shock to complete the Russian Revolution's heptad. Or the two revolutions might be successfully put together as the two shocks of a

* We say essentially, because on the scale of the history of a great nation there must always be existential exceptions of offence, but the "woe to those by whom they come" can only be by the product of Jefferson's recommended policy of eternal vigilance practiced by a productive citizenry.

revolution by a Deng, a Rajiv Gandhi, a Sadat-cum-Nasser, or an insightful Brazilian, Mexican, Argentine, or European. The absence of any manager of requisite national power thoroughly structuring this clear possibility shows the difficulty of attaining to a heptadic structural approach. It shows the difficulty because of course the reward of historical immortality is high enough to motivate the intensest interest, and to a degree Roosevelt's New Deal, Kennedy's New Frontier and Khrushev's Thaw represented a beginning that soon reached unrealized personal difficulties and stopped.

If a Soviet leader should adopt an approach that would allow the C shock of inalienable rights, he might find that revolution's D shock to higher value for the greater world to a great extent within the USSR spiritual traditions themselves, Gogol, Dostoyevsky, Tolstoy, Kandinsky, Mendeleev, Tsiolkovsky, Vernadsky, Stanislavsky, Meyerhold, the deep Georgian, Armenian, and Sufi (genuine, not the emotionalist fanatics) traditions of the Southlands, and shamanic wisdom of the Northlands and Asian steppes.

As stated, if the manager of at least one of these two great heptadic efforts do not make such-efforts, then new efforts must arise, perhaps already have arisen in the Chou En-lai/Deng tradition in China, the Nehruvian line in India, which will pick up the pieces that American and Russian managers could not bring themselves to do.

After all, if Pan-American wouldn't move on to the next step, then People's Express steps in for its moment in the sun. If the Post Office won't do it, telex, modems, and Federal Express take the problem to the next step. And if the American and Russian leaders can't move on to the next step from inalienable rights or mass participation, then someone else will do it because that's the next step. The unfinished American and Russian Revolutions hold the entire world's historical agenda at a stop. Maybe some manager will figure how to do it on a non-nation-state basis.

The structure of *succeed* is, whether or not a manager uses it or whether any manager of a given epoch uses it. Structural mathematics does not depend on existence, but existence can always profit by the conscious use of structural mathematics. And since values are infinite, the structure of succeed opens up possibilities for infinite evolution within the finite existential world.

Try the exercise:

(1) Work out the interest you have in the transformational effort. Of course, you must satisfy yourself that you are beginning with at least one hexad, a genuine event, although you will need seven of them.

Change occurs at every structural level, but transformational change only at this level. And only a small percentage of monads contain even the potential for a seven-fold structure. A manager who wishes to work at world-historic levels will never waste his attention on a monad of less potential even if he does not carry it so far for years.

Notes

(2) Set up the scale of seven with numbers and names. Leave two spaces to allow for hazard X and C, and for D.
(3) Now put in the actual content of your *realization of personal difficulties* and also for the other six names.
(4) Work out the dyadic intensity of the 21 dyads: *interest* and *applying that interest to yourself, interest* and *picking up the pieces* and so on. At least the key 1-4-7 triad should be thoroughly investigated and brought into line with the strategy adopted triadic stage, or if it is now seen that strategy will not bring about transformation, to revise that strategy. Because of the time needed for transformation, you may have to work out a sequence of strategies.
(5) You should work out the number of productive systems that it takes to make a heptad, and how many significant organizations. One man I know in the UK has, for example, 9 at least potentially significant non-profit corporations that he controls in order to mount his effort toward transformation of a certain situation.
(6) By inspection one can see that seven events are mathematically possible, for example: 123456 and 134567. These are not to be confused with the names of the seven, but represent the six existential dimensions: so seven events must be fully realized to make a heptadic transformation. But one event must be chosen to commence the process in time although all the events must resonate with each other.
(7) The shocks C and D call for a special treatment since they "come from outside" but in a reinforcing direction. Are you structuring an openness to such necessities? "They also serve who only stand and wait" might well be Milton's description of such a point on the heptad. One rushes ahead only to transformation "downwards", failure, not "upwards", succeed. Heptads are not horizontal structures, "more", but vertical structures, evolution, or involution.
(8) Contemplate your results. Do not expect to apply any of what you have structured directly because what you have structured is your thought not the outside world. Your thought will now be in the process of aligning with all the necessities of action in your managerial sphere. Your thought will cease being the opponent of your actions, but your actions will not cease experiencing opposition. Above all, for goodness sake, do not issue any directives couched in structural thought terms or start-up pseudo-democratic discussion groups about structural thought or you will promote only a new and very dull hypocrisy. Remember, please, that subordinates will use piously any phraseology thought to be necessary to maintain good relations with "the boss". Whether in the case of Catholic “theology", Marxist "ideology", free enterprise

"doctrine", or structures treated as "formula", such behavior only results in a waste of time, a distortion of relationship, and an ache in the heart. Benefits will accrue, but they will come because of the synergy of your attentive thought with your external actions, not because of your handing on digested at best, vomited at worst, pabulum.

Notes

Notes

REVIEW

(1) Go back to the monad and make any changes you now deem necessary.

(2) Advance forward then to the dyad, triad, tetrad, pentad, hexad, and heptad, making any changes you deem necessary.

(3) This critical review should be repeated until no great new insights are constated (meaning registered on your sensorium and verified by logical scrutiny).

You have now structured by the method of successive approximations what can be called *managerial thought*. If you are a practicing manager, you have structured your thought in such a way that your thinking will assist you to *succeed*. The study of and work with these structures will inculcate humility as well as create new confidence because their study, particularly the structure of seven, show thought how dramatically dangerous indeed the cosmos is to the achievement of intention however backed by heart's desire. But then the rare has always been the supreme prize. And this rare *succeed* also benefits all within the reach of its domain, and links with all the other *succeeds* to make *reality,* that fabulous all-at-once ever-creative alignment of the actual, the potential, the possible, and the lawfully-excluded, or impossible.

APPENDIX

For those managers who wish the philosophical reasoning behind adopting a structural or successive approximations approach in order to live more deeply in reality.

If reality were an absolute, then the first effort we should make should be to attain to a knowledge of the absolute, since we could then derive all necessary partial knowledge from that absolute knowledge. From this belief have been formed the various theologies, most notably the Aquinas theology of Roman Catholicism, and ideologies, most notably the Leninist ideology of the Soviet Union. The study of *the* God (the Creator), or *the* idea (dialectical materialism) tells us all we could wish to know about how to deal with the price for shoes, the status of women, what to do about social injustice, and how we should educate ourselves, and to what end we should make these various efforts. History shows that no theology or ideology makes a good manager, however, although indeed good managers of a theology or ideology do arise from time to time.

Structural thought commences from a different place: *experience.*

If the full experience of man makes an adequate sample of the cosmos, then we must recognize that uncertainty and relativity, not absolutes, gather about our intentions in our search for truth. The cosmos that we inhabit becomes fundamentally not only unknown, but unknowable, possibilities or a caravan of dreams rather than the working out of a cosmic plan, those succeeding who go with the plan, and those failing, of course, who oppose the plan.

Now if it is true that ultimately we possess not revelation of the absolute but rather revelations from experience as our guide then we immediately meet two major limitations that sentence us to uncertainty, relativity, and danger (there may be indeed be other limitations in the cosmos itself that eventuate in further uncertainty, relativity, and danger):

(1) the perceptions that make up the database for our experience have evolved to cover only a small percentage of the range of phenomena, for example sight receives about 1% of the range of electromagnetic radiation, and not only of the range but also of direction, sight being restricted to two "slits" more or less "straight ahead", and approximately the same holds true for hearing, taste, smells, and

touches. Even when instrumentation expands our perception range, the directional aspects, the lapses of memory, the inablility to imaginatively combine percepts beyond a certain level of complexity, the limited energy for "reflection", the interferences of language with common sense, and a relatively short lifetime constrain our maximum potential experience of the universe to a small fractional component of reality.

(2) the forms of thought by which we "work upon" the perceptual data base are frighteningly error-prone. Associative thought can be interrupted or "censored" by the smallest emotionally imbedded pain or physiological stiffness, the "trauma" or "engram", and our mind divided into at least two regions unaware of each other, the so-called "conscious" and so-called "subconscious" minds. In other words every human being is to a degree "schizophrenic", or of two minds about anything. A man who overcomes this handicap is considered the rarest of the rare, called a "great artist", a "Zen master" or "sage", so exceptional is his achievement. Logic we know operates only upon its own premises, and therefore can never be better than its basic assumption, or "divinity". So all of us have seen that the too-logical man always fails by "pushing things too far", "he lacks common-sense", "he hasn't got the sense God gave a little green crabapple". The dialectic of Plato, Hegel, and Marx with its mechanical expansionism, thesis, anti-thesis, synthesis becoming the new thesis, anti-thesis, into a new synthesis, on and on, in no way enables one to escape the assumption trap of logic, though it makes the results subtler by confronting the first gratuitous assumption with its opposite and having them fight it out. In short, what is chosen as the first thesis must remain "divine", "accepted", or the dialectical operation must come to a halt just as the logical.

It is true that the scientific method by a judicious study of perceptions and limiting the choice of thesis to be deduced from the perceived facts (hypothesis) and then proceeding via logic or dialectics as far as deduction can travel, then checking predictions as to the world of fact from those deductions to begin afresh the process, enables progress to be made in the control of the worlds of physics, chemistry, geology, and genetics, but complex systems on the order of civilization and history which involve interest and intention remain beyond its help, and scientists are usually the first to admit they have an incomplete idea as to the consequences of their discoveries, or of the best uses for them.

Nonetheless science, having expanded our field of knowledge of reality by its specialist methods, gave a great hope to thinkers and leaders of the nineteenth and early twentieth centuries that specialization of scientific functions would create a high road to a perception of *total reality* by addition of a truth here and a truth there. They thought that if sufficient specialties were operating, the specialist knowledges would lead to an understanding of *objective reality,* and by objective meant much the same thing as by the old "absolute". The idea prospered that each new scientific advance brought us one step nearer knowledge of *objective reality,* added another brick to the edifice.

The world wars, world depressions, world revolutions, world balance of terror, and world devastation of the biosphere have put paid to such hopes that a close study of the limitations of perceptions and forms of thought would enable man to attain to absolute certainty from his experience. In fact, the uncertainties added by the growth of science themselves dealt the mortal blow to such an easy but destructive hope.

One method remains: that of *number* or authentic metaphysics. Numbers have properties that produce particular kinds of knowledge. Pythagoras and Plato who reportedly learned this from Egyptian priests-mathematicians long ago explicitly pointed out some of these properties that can be seen implicit in the symbols of ancient Egypt, that three thousand year long *succeed* until devastated by the ferocious armies of Cambyses the Mad. The number 1 for example contains the property of sameness, the number 2 of difference, and the number 3 of ratio, proportion, or relationship.

A progressive, ever-deepening approach to reality became possible.

This book contains an account of how the progression of *number* can be applied to the thought about the management of enterprise of any kind whatsoever. The reflective reader will, of course, see that *number* could be in principle, if he but knew how in practice, applied to his life and even to human destiny.

Equally, to reflection it will be clear that this method while assisting greatly the development of practical capacity to deal with the manifold uncertainty, relativity, and danger that active life in the milieu of the space biosphere epoch cannot but acknowledge, will never and can never give "the answer". The method can help prepare the actor who then must go on the stage of the dramatically dangerous universe, there "to be or not to be" depending upon the ever-changing uncertain and relative response to his ever-changing uncertain and relative attention. "Readiness is all."

Other publications from Synergetic Press

BIOSPHERICS

Space Biospheres

by John Allen and Mark Nelson

A compelling vision of a possible future which moves the dream of the space frontier from the realms of science fiction into the practical domain of science and management. $6.95/£4.95

The Biosphere Catalogue

Editor in Chief, T.P. Snyder
Scientific Editor, John Allen

A comprehensive presentation of the biosphere, with contributions from over thirty leading figures in fields ranging from atmosphere, hydrosphere, geosphere, plants and animals to cultures, cities, space biospheres, genetics and travel. $12.95/£9.95

The Biosphere

by V.I. Vernadsky
The first English edition of the classic work by Vernadsky originally published in Russian in 1926. $5.95/£3.95

Feng-Shui

by Ernest J. Eitel
with commentary by John Michell

The science of sacred landscape in old China. The first English treatise ever written on the Chinese code of practice used in overall matters of architectural design, city planning and use of the countryside. $5.95/£3.95

FICTION

39 Blows On A Gone Trumpet

by Johnny Dolphin

Dolphin, the latest to emerge from the Tangier school of writing. Captivating prose that swings with its own rhythm, 39 riffs sounding unique historical beats of Manhattan, Iran, and Tangier. $5.95/£4.50

POETRY

On Feet of Gold

by Ira Cohen

Selected poetry. Catharsis and prophesy are combined through incisive and penetrating imagery of man as he is, in contrast to the poet's vision of man as he might be. (forthcoming)

The Dream and Drink of Freedom

by Johnny Dolphin
Introduction by Kathelin Hoffman

Selected poems written between 1948 and 1986. The poems chronicle both a personal and social history of essence America where eternal vigilance is the price of liberty. (forthcoming)

DRAMA

The Collected Works of the Caravan of Dreams Theater: Volume I and II

Volume I includes Caravan's adaptations/translations of three classic dramas, *Gilgamesh, Marouf the Cobbler,* and *Faust: Part One;* Volume II contains three original plays of modern times, *Billy the Kid, Metal Woman, Tin Can Man.* $5.95/£3.95

Kabuki Blues Comic

Conceived and Illustrated by Corinna MacNeice
Based on Caravan of Dreams Theater production.

Exciting new strokes in comic books. $1.50/ £1.00